CLEVELAND RADIO PLAYERS

Published by Cleveland Radio Players

Copyright © 2015 by Milton Matthew Horowitz

All rights, including the right of reproduction in whole or in part, in any form, including digital reproduction, are reserved. Published in the United States by Cleveland Radio Players.

CAUTION: Professionals and amateurs are hereby warned that *Stealing Lincoln*, being fully protected under the Copyright Laws of the United States is subject to royalty. All rights, including professional, amateur, motion picture, recitation, lecturing, public reading, radio and television broadcasting, and the rights of translation into foreign languages, are strictly reserved. Particular emphasis is laid on the question of readings, permission for which must be secured in writing from the author's representative at Cleveland Radio Players, 2218 Superior Ave, Suite 203, Cleveland, OH 44114. The amateur acting rights of *Stealing Lincoln* are controlled exclusively for the author by the author's representative.

ISBN 978-0692389492 (Cleveland Radio Players, The)

Original Adaption and Performances

Originally adapted for the radio and performed by The Cleveland Radio Players. Directed by Milton Matthew Horowitz. Recorded at Bad Racket Studios.

Starring:
(in order of appearance)

Robert Branch	Abraham Lincoln
Jack Matuszewski	Lincoln Honor Guard
Denny Castiglione	Father
Giovanni Castiglione	Son
Llenelle Gibson	Daughter
Robert Branch	James "Big Jim" Kenally
Cody Zack	Terrence Mullen
Charles Hargrave	Jack Hughes
Logan Smith	Lewis Swegel
Milton Horowitz	Patrick D. Tyrrelle
David Flynt	Billy Brown
	Train Conductor
Cory Shy	Secret Service Agent

Stealing Lincoln

Milton Matthew Horowitz

The Cleveland Radio Players
2218 Superior Ave #203
Cleveland Ohio 44114

www.clevelandradioplayers.com
theradioplayers@gmail.com
2162694171

CAST OF CHARACTERS

>ABRAHAM LINCOLN
The once-president of the United States of America

>LINCOLN HONOR GUARD
The tour guide that speaks at the Lincoln Monument in Oakridge Cemetery

>FATHER
Father of a family on an educational vacation

>SON
Bratty kid on vacation

>DAUGHTER
Bratty kid on vacation

>JAMES "BIG JIM" KENNALLY
An Irish immigrant and counterfeit ringleader

>TERRENCE MULLEN
Another Irish immigrant and a member of Big Jim's gang, 28 years old

>JACK HUGHES
Friend of Terrence Mullen and counterfeiter in Big Jim's gang

>LEWIS SWEGEL
A wise-cracking chap who'd been busted a few times for horse thievery

>BILLY BROWN
The get-away driver hired by Lewis Swegel and the Secret Service to infiltrate the counterfeiting gang

>PATRICK D. TYRRELL
An Irish American detective of the United States Secret Service who, as head of the field office in Chicago, became involved in foiling a plot to steal the remains of President Abraham Lincoln on November 7, 1876

> TRAIN CONDUCTOR
> Literally says "All aboard" and "All aboard that's comin' aboard," and that's it!

> SECRET SERVICE AGENT
> One of the first agents hired to the secret service in charge of a group of Pinkerton detectives

OPENING CREDITS

> THE VOICE OF THE CLEVELAND RADIO PLAYERS
> Hello... This is the voice of The Cleveland Radio Players... My name is Denny Castiglione, ladies and gentlemen,

OPENING FANFARE

> and you're listening to The Cleveland Radio Players performance of STEALING LINCOLN. Written and directed by Milton Matthew Horowitz. Narrated by Jack Matuszewski.

ACT 1

SCENE 1

EXT. THE GETTYSBURG ADDRESS

HAIL TO THE CHIEF

PATRIOTIC MUSIC

> ABRAHAM LINCOLN
> Four score and seven years ago our fathers brought forth on this continent, a new nation, conceived in Liberty, and dedicated to the proposition that all men are created equal... This nation, under God, shall have a new birth of freedom-- and that government of the people, by the people, for the people, shall not perish from the earth...

CROWD CHEERING EXUBERANTLY

FADE OUT PATRIOTIC MUSIC

EXT. THE LINCOLN MEMORIAL DAY

                CROWD CHEERS TURN TO A MILD CLAP
                        FADE IN PUBLIC PARK ENVIRONMENT

                    LINCOLN GUARD OF HONOR
          ...And that, my friends... Was the
          famous words spoken by Abraham
          Lincoln at the Gettysburg
          address... It wouldn't be for
          another two years that President
          Lincoln would be fatally shot with
          a 44. caliber derringer at the Ford
          theater by John Wilkes Booth,
          before being carried to the Peters'
          house where he would later die...
          And that concludes our tour of the
          Lincoln tomb today... Thank you so
          much for visiting the Oakridge
          Cemetary. Thousands of people come
          to Springfield each year to visit
          the tomb and the Lincoln Guard of
          Honor thanks you...

                    FATHER
          Ya hear that, kids?... Inspiring,
          isn't it?

                    SON
          Yeah, dad, real inspiring.

                    DAUGHTER
          Dad, can we go back to the hotel
          now?

                    FATHER
          Look kids, we didn't drive all the
          way here for you two to sit in the
          hotel and order room service...

                    DAUGHTER
          But dad, it's just sooooo boring.

                    LINCOLN GUARD OF HONOR
          I heard that...

                    SON
          Yeah, dad... This place sucks...
          And the tour guide is a snore
          monger.

                    LINCOLN GUARD OF HONOR
          I'm standing right over here...

                    FATHER
          Look, I paid good money for you
          kids to learn something on this
          trip, and by God, you're gonna
          learn something, no matter how
          boring the tour guide is!

                    LINCOLN GUARD OF HONOR
          Still standing... Right over
          here...

                    FATHER
          Look Mr. Tour guide... You got any
          stories that are a little more
          exciting... I mean, one that my
          kids might find fascinating.

                    LINCOLN GUARD OF HONOR
          Well, if you don't find the
          founding of the greatest nation in
          history exciting, then I don't know
          what is!

                    FATHER
          Well, I mean, of course it's
          exciting... Nothing more exciting
          than patriotism if you ask me...
          But... My kids sir... They're all
          affected by the internet age... You
          got any thing a bit more juicy...
          Something with some action or
          suspense, maybe?

                    LINCOLN GUARD OF HONOR
          Well... There is this one story ...
          But... I don't know... It's maybe
          not so suitable for children...

                    FATHER
          Oh... Well then, maybe you
          shouldn't.

                    SON
          Aww, c'mon dad... I'm old enough.

                    DAUGHTER
          Yeah, dad, you're gonna have to
          stop treating us like kids and
          censoring everything we hear... I
          already kiss boys... On the lips!

SON
Eww gross.

FATHER
That's enough... Okay, start with the story already.

LINCOLN GUARD OF HONOR
Oh well, um, okay, well, here we go here... Uh... Four score and seven years agooo...

SON
Ugh... We heard that part already!

LINCOLN GUARD OF HONOR
Ok, ok... Fine... But did you know that once... counterfeiters hatched a plot to steal the dead body of President Lincoln and hold it for ransom?

DAUGHTER
Ewww, gross!

SON
No way... cool.

FATHER
Oh c'mon now, that can't be true!

LINCOLN GUARD OF HONOR
Oh, but it is, sir... I assure you... Ya see... President Lincoln was great man, but also a hated man in many parts of the South... It's not easy to lead a country during a civil war...

FATHER
Tell me about it... I had to deal with a civil war the whole ride here...

DAUGHTER
Dad, he's doing that thing with his gum again...

SON
Shut up!

FATHER
Knock it off, you two, and listen to the boring tour guide story now... Or we're going to another museum or monument, GOT IT!?

LINCOLN GUARD OF HONOR
Um... Ok... That's offensive... Well, just keep moving on... Ya see... The story of how Presidents Lincoln's body was stolen really starts before he was killed... Abraham Lincoln had a plan to save this great nation and unite us once again... Only thing was the South hated the terms he was proposing...

SON
What were the terms?

LINCOLN GUARD OF HONOR
Well... He not only set the slaves free but he also decreed that all men be given a fair day's wage... Great news for the slaves, however, these new financial changes would ultimately put an end to the plantation era in America...

DAUGHTER
You mean, not everyone wanted to end slavery? Why not?! Slavery is... Just wrong!

LINCOLN GUARD OF HONOR
Indeed it is, young lady, however... Many of the plantation owners feared they would lose their businesses to freeing their slaves or even paying them a fair wage.

SON
Last time I checkedm that was called racism.

FATHER
That's right, son...

LINCOLN GUARD OF HONOR
Yes, that is right son... Now if you don't mind... As it were, many people hated President Lincoln. And to get back at him for making them

LINCOLN GUARD OF HONOR
pay their slaves... Well... They
started counterfeiting money...

SON
No wayyyy... Did they get caught?

LINCOLN GUARD OF HONOR
Of course they did... In fact...
Putting an end to counterfeiting
rings was the job of a special task
force that President Lincoln put in
place that would one day become the
Secret Service!

FATHER
See, I told you the boring tour
guide would have some interesting
information... You just have to
ask, kids...

LINCOLN GUARD OF HONOR
Still... Very... Offensive...
Anyways... President Lincoln's men
were investigating an Irish crime
boss by the name of James "Big Jim"
Kennally... They had very little to
go on in making an arrest for Big
Jim, however, they were able to
catch up with his engraver Benjamin
Boyd, who'd been arrested and
sentenced to ten years at the
Illinois State Penitentiary in
Joliet.

FATHER
Ya see kids, crime doesn't pay.

LINCOLN GUARD OF HONOR
YES CRIME DOES NOT PAY!... Now if
you please, just let me finish...
Big Jim had very little experience
in body snatching... You see, this
plan involved the kidnapping of
Lincoln's dead body, so Big Jim
Kennally recruited two members of
his gang, Terrence Mullen and Jack
Hughes, to carry out the plot. They
discussed their plans at "the Hub",
a saloon on Madison Street in
Chicago...

FADE OUT ENVIRONMENT

SCENE 2 INT. THE HUB TAVERN

CROSS FADE IN "THE HUB" ENVIRONMENT

LINCOLN GUARD OF HONOR
This flash back scenario begins with a bunch of pissed off drunks sitting around the poker table in an ale house, talking slight against the way things have been since Lincoln freed the slaves.

TERRENCE MULLEN
October 1876!

BIG JIM
Why did you just say that out loud?

TERRENCE MULLEN
Say what?

BIG JIM
October 1876?

TERRENCE MULLEN
Oh... Just in case someone was eavesdropping and was wondering what year it is...

BIG JIM
Uh, huh?... That got me thinking... You know it's been over two years since that since that republican put that anti-counterfeiting team into effect and put an end to our work... I can't believe its already been two years.

TERRENCE MULLEN
Seems like just yesterday he was shot... Too bad Mr. Boothe didn't shoot him before he had Ben arrested.

BIG JIM
You're right... It's a damn shame... He was the best engraver on either side of the Mason-Dixon line... And now look... The only decoration in this entire bar is a bust of Abe Lincoln's stupid face lookin' over us like a evil specter... While Boyd sits in jail.

JACK HUGHES
The only thing worse would be
puttin' Abe Lincoln's face on
money... It's too bad Big Jim...
Ben does not deserve to be sittin'
in that State Penitentiary in
Joliet... He was a good man... His
father raised him right. It's not
his fault he fell into tough
times...

BIG JIM
Better him than us.. But you're
right... If we had Boyd back we
might be able to get back to
counterfieting.

TERRENCE MULLEN
I can't believe Boyd got 10 years
for counterfeiting... You should
watch out, Jim, I'm sure they're
looking for you too!

BIG JIM
Ha... I'd like to see them try... I
can smell copper from a mile
away... Lincoln's stupid Secret
Service cost me plenty of money the
last two years and I aim to settle
the score...

JACK HUGHES
How are you expectin' to do that
Jim? They must have cost you 'round
200 thousand dollars in fake money
at this point.

TERRENCE MULLEN
You'd have to kidnap Lincoln
himself to collect that kind of
ransom!

TERRENCE AND JACK LAUGHING

BIG JIM
What did you just say?

TERRENCE MULLEN
I said to get that kind of ransom
you'd have to kidnap Lincoln
himself.

BIG JIM
That's it!

JACK HUGHES
Whats it?

BIG JIM
Kidnapping Lincoln!

TERRENCE AND JACK LAUGHING

TERRENCE MULLEN
How ya gonna do that Jim, hmm? The man's been dead eleven years!

BIG JIM
That's just it!... He's been dead eleven years... Nobody's guarding his tomb in Springfield... No watchmen or Pinkertons... The graveyard is literally a ghost town... There's a national treasure right under their noses and I aim to snatch it up and collect!

JACK HUGHES
I don't know if he's drunk or crazy...

BIG JIM
Gentlemen... This is gonna be the easiest robbery in the history of the world...

TERRENCE MULLEN
That sounds great, Jim, only one thing... We don't have any experience in bodysnatching, now, do we?

FOOTSTEPS

LINCOLN GUARD OF HONOR
It was at this very moment that Lewis Swegel, an ex-con, would overhear the conversation of Big Jim Kennally and his counterfeit ring.

LEWIS SWEGEL
(clears throat)
Excuse me... But did you lot just say you were needing the service of a credible body snatcher?

BIG JIM
...What's it to you?

TERRENCE MULLEN
Yeah, who the hell are you?

LEWIS SWEGEL
Why, I'm "The Boss Body Snatcher of Chicago,"... That's who the hell I am!

BIG JIM
The... what?

JACK HUGHES
I didn't know Chicago had a "Boss Body Snatcher," did you know that, Terrence?

TERRENCE MULLEN
Well, I never knew, to be honest.

BIG JIM
Please, Mr... uhh...

LEWIS SWEGEL
Swegel is the name... Lewis Swegel!

BIG JIM
Mr. Swegel... Would you please enlighten us as to how it is that you have come to be the Boss Body Snatcher of Chicago?

LEWIS SWEGEL
Of course... Ya see... Robbing graves is a lucrative business in 19th century America.

TERRENCE MULLEN
Lucrative, you say?

LEWIS SWEGEL
Certainly!

JACK HUGHES
How so?

LEWIS SWEGEL
Well, the thing is, medical schools these days want cadavers for dissection in their anatomy classes... And they pay reasonably well for fresh bodies.

                    BIG JIM
          Is that so?... How is it you've
          gotten away with it for this long?

                    LEWIS SWEGEL
          Well, it's not easy... These thefts
          ain't greeted happily... I've seen
          mobs of citizens outraged by the
          body snatchings that end up
          attacking medical schools and
          doctor's offices in revenge.

                    TERRENCE MULLEN
          What?!

                    LEWIS SWEGEL
          Yeah, I seen it happen in New York
          City, Baltimore, New Haven, and
          Cleveland... That's when I got
          smart and moved to Chicago and
          became--

                    BIG JIM
          The Boss Body Snatcher of
          Chicago... Now I've heard
          everything...

                    LEWIS SWEGEL
          Oh, a nay-sayer, huh? Well, fine...
          I know when I'm not appreciated...

                    BIG JIM
          Wait, wait, wait... C'mon now, let
          us hear you out.

                    LEWIS SWEGEL
          Well I overhear that you need a
          body snatcher, and I just so happen
          to be an expert in that area of
          work. So what are we talking about
          here, huh? Whose body is it you
          wanna snatch, huh?

                    BIG JIM
          Lincoln.

                    LEWIS SWEGEL
          Did you say...

                    TERRENCE MULLEN
          He said Lincoln...

                    LEWIS SWEGEL
Uh huh...

                    JACK HUGHES
As in President Lincoln...

                    LEWIS SWEGEL
I see...

                    BIG JIM
What's-a matter, son?... Too much
trouble for the Boss Body Snatcher
of Chicago?

                    LEWIS SWEGEL
No... Not at all... It's just, with
a job like that... It's gonna take
careful preparation and precise
planning to pull it off...

                    BIG JIM
So you're sayin' you think you can
steal the body of Lincoln, and get
away with it without being seen or
outraging any citizens?

                    LEWIS SWEGEL
Certainly... We just need to make
sure we have all our contingencies
planned.

                    TERRENCE MULLEN
Where we gonna hide the body,
Jim?... Huh?... You know anybody
gonna let you stash away the stolen
president's dead body?

                    BIG JIM
Maybe we don't need anybody's
help... Where could we hide a
body?...

                    JACK HUGHES
...Maybe we could stash his body in
the dunes near Lake Michigan? The
wind will cover up any trace of the
body being buried or the tracks we
might make in the process!

                    BIG JIM
That's brilliant Jack!... We have
the who, and the what, and where.
Now all we have to do is decide

BIG JIM
what terms we want for the release of his body... Let's see here...

TERRENCE MULLEN
Why don't you ask to spring Boyd out of the big house...

BIG JIM
That's right... If we get Boyd back, we can make ourselves all the money we want... But, just in case, we'll ask for 200 thousand dollars too... It's a nice round number.

JACK HUGHES
Jim, do you really think they'll pay 200 thousand dollars for the return of Lincoln's corpse?

BIG JIM
Even if we just get them to pardon Benjamin Boyd we can go back to work like we use to, and counterfeit fifty dollar bills instead of nickles...

TERRENCE MULLEN
That's all I needed to hear...I'm in.

JACK HUGHES
Yeah alright, if Terrence is in, then I'm in...

BIG JIM
And what about you, Mr. Swegel?... You want a little piece of this action?...

LEWIS SWEGEL
They don't call me The Boss Body Snatcher of Chicago for nothin'... Now let me just get this straight and go over this one last time... The plan is to steal Lincoln's body from its sarcophagus... Bury it in the dunes near Lake Michigan... Then hold it ransom in exchange for a full pardon of Benjamin Boyd the engraver, and 200 thousand dollars in cash...

BIG JIM
Sounds about right... Men?

TERRENCE MULLEN
Aye...

JACK HUGHES
Aye...

LEWIS SWEGEL
Now, like I said, a job of this caliber is gonna take precision timing... We have to plan this just right... At a time that nobody will be guarding the tomb or graveyard.

BIG JIM
I got it... Election night. ...It's just around the corner and every proper man will be at the polls like the cattle they are... All their houses will be empty, and I bet the honor guard will be absent as well... It's not like a crime of this kind has happened before... Like I said... It'll be the easiest robbery in the history of the world...

EVERYONE LAUGHS

BIG JIM
I think more drinks are in order... Bartender! Come down here!

DRINKS ON TABLE
BEER POURING

EVERYONE LAUGHS

BIG JIM
It's plans like this that deserve a toast... To Lewis Swegal... The Boss Body Snatcher of Chicago... What good fortune that we would meet you on this day...

CHEERS!

GLASSES CLINK

LINCOLN GUARD OF HONOR
Ironically Swegals was an undercover informant for the Secret Service... Unknown by Big Jim and

LINCOLN GUARD OF HONOR
the gang, their plot was already doomed before it started, so Swegals says...

LEWIS SWEGEL
Look guys, if we're gonna do this right, we're gonna need a getaway driver and I got just the guy for the job... His name is Billy Brown... I'm gonna go recruit him and meet back up with you guys tomorrow.

LINCOLN GUARD OF HONOR
Swegel would recruit a getaway driver by the name of Billy Brown. However, upon leaving the bar he went straight to the local chief of the Secret Service to tell him of the crazy plot.

FADE OUT "THE HUB" ENVIRONMENT
FADE IN PUBLIC ENVIRONMENT

SON
Wait? Why would Swegel want to turn in Big Jim like that?

DAUGHTER
Yeah? What did Big Jim ever do to Swegel?

LINCOLN GUARD OF HONOR
Well, nothing really, he was just in the wrong place at the wrong time talking about the wrong thing... You see, Swegel and his friend Billy Brown were horse thieves, only they weren't very good at it... they'd been arrested many times and were out on parole as paid informants of the local Secret Service chief, Patrick D. Tyrrell.

FADE OUT ENVIRONMENT

SCENE 3 INT. PATRICK D. TYRRELLS OFFICE

FADE IN SCENE MUSIC

          LINCOLN GUARD OF HONOR
Swegel spilled his guts about the whole plot, hoping he would simply be paid for his information. However, the Secret Service was in the business of stopping counterfeiters, not body snatchers... So back at Patrick's office...

          PATRICK D. TYRRELL
It's a completely DAMNABLE ACT if you ask me... I am horrified by the implication of this crime. It should be considered an act of NATIONAL IMPORTANCE!

          LEWIS SWEGEL
Well, that's what we thought, sir... That's why I reckon I'd tell you as just as soon as I could.

          PATRICK D. TYRRELL
I have one question for you, Swegel... How the hell did you get them to trust you enough to tell you about their heinous plot?

          LEWIS SWEGEL
I told them I'm the Boss Body Snatcher of Chicago.

          PATRICK D. TYRRELL
The what?

          LEWIS SWEGEL
I don't know. I made it up.

          PATRICK D. TYRRELL
Well, good work, Swegel... I have a meeting tomorrow with the late President's only living son, Robert, tomorrow... I will indeed inform him of this awful crime and make sure these crooks are brought to justice...

LEWIS SWEGEL
Great!... So you can just go ahead and pay me my reward for snitching and I'll be on my way!

PATRICK D. TYRRELL
... I'm sorry, it's not going to be that easy this time, Lewis... I'm gonna have to ask you to do one more thing for me before I can pay you.

LEWIS SWEGEL
Well, what's that?

PATRICK D. TYRRELL
You and that friend of yours, Billy Brown, are to going to have to help Big Jim's boys pull off this ridiculous crime.

LEWIS SWEGEL
What! Why the hell would you want me to do that?!

PATRICK D. TYRRELL
It's a matter of technical legalities... I can't just go over there and arrest Jim and his boys just for gettin' drunk and talkin' slight against the once-president on your word and your word alone... And furthermore, the Secret Service was put in place to catch counterfeiters, not grave robbers... But I suspect once I inform Robert Lincoln of the despicable crime, he will grant me permission to place other Secret Service agents at the scene of the crime prior to the heist, and thwart the would-be crooks in the middle of the act... We just need you to lead them there and act as their cohorts... What say you, Swegel?

LEWIS SWEGEL
Well, I think it sounds crazy, sir... I thought Big Jim's idea was crazy... But this is just--

PATRICK D. TYRRELL
The Secret Service needs your help Lewis, your country need your help... This is your chance to shed your identity as a horse thief and be remembered as a hero!

LEWIS SWEGEL
Well, gee, when you put it like that...

PATRICK D. TYRRELL
That's what I thought... Now listen... You're to travel by train with Hughes and Mullen to Lincoln's tomb in Illinois. In the meantime, I will be in contact with the former President's Son and the Illinois Secret Service to set up and anti-bodysnatching sting.

LEWIS SWEGEL
You know how ridiculous that sounds, right?... And I'm gonna get paid extra for this when it's all over, right?

PATRICK D. TYRRELL
Son... They may even pin a medal on you.

LINCOLN GUARD OF HONOR
Ridiculous or not, Swegel would accept the terms of the job... Provided he would be compensated handsomely for going along with the ruse of stealing Lincoln's corpse for ransom.

FADE ENVIRONMENT

SCENE 4 EXT LINCOLN MEMORIAL

FADE IN PUBLIC ENVIRONMENT

LINCOLN GUARD OF HONOR
And, well, that just about wraps it up! The rest is history as they say...

SON
Wait, what?

> DAUGHTER
> That can't be the end of the story...?

> SON
> Yeah, what about the heist?

> LINCOLN GUARD OF HONOR
> Oh, not so boring now, am I?... Yeah that's what I thought... Snore monger, he says... You know what, you better take that back now or I'm not gonna tell the rest of the story.

> SON
> Ok fine... I'm sorry I called you a snore monger.

> FATHER
> See, I told you kids this would be fun...

> LINCOLN GUARD OF HONOR
> Please don't interrupt sir... Now where were we?... Oh, the train ride to Lincoln's tomb... Right.

FADE IN TRAIN STATION SOUNDS

> LINCOLN GUARD OF HONOR
> On November 2... Robert Lincoln approved Tyrrell's request to act based on the information... Tyrrell then recruited a group of Secret Service agents to spring a trap on the would-be grave robbers.

SCENE 5 INT. TRAIN STATION

> LINCOLN GUARD OF HONOR
> Ya see, Big Jim Kennally was more of an idea man than an actual laboring crook... So he sent his four men, Terrance Mullan, Jack Hughes, Lewis Swegel, and getaway driver Billy Brown, on November 6th, 1876.

TRAIN WHISTLE SOUND

TRAIN CONDUCTOR
All ABOARD!

PATRICK D. TYRRELL
Here's your tickets... You two are to travel by train from here to Springfield, where the late president is buried... There will be other agents on the train, so know that you are in safe hands should trouble arise... You won't know who these men are, to make sure your cover isn't accidentally blown... But they know to trail you and wait for the word.

LEWIS SWEGEL
Look, no trouble's gonna rise, because as soon as they heft Lincoln's coffin, I'm gonna holler the secret word that cues the cavalry to come in and make the arrest...

PATRICK D. TYRRELL
That's right... Now remember the word is "wash"... And you, Billy Brown... Your main goal here is to just act as a getaway driver for Lewis... That's it... Try to do as little talking as possible.

BILLY BROWN
I gotcha boss... 'cept one thing... I don't rightly have no carriage to drive...

LEWIS SWEGEL
Aww shoot... I forgot about that... How we gonna make a getaway with no getaway carriage.

PATRICK D. TYRRELL
Look, just steal one when you get into town... You're thieves, aren't ya? Well, make use of your skills... I'll pardon any crimes you commit, so long as they are in the name of saving the former president's body from scandal...

LEWIS SWEGEL
Aye... Make sure your boys don't trail too closely... I don't want to be called a traiter or a snitch... C'mon Billy... Mullen and Hughes will be here any minute... We're suppose to meet 'em in the first train car.

FOOTSTEPS X2

LINCOLN GUARD OF HONOR
It was at this very time that Secret Service would be watching Swegel's every move... He walked over to the first car where Mullen and Hughs were waiting.

TERRENCE MULLEN
Alright, train's 'bout to leave, let's wait till the last second before we board... Make sure we weren't followed...

JACK HUGHES
You boys weren't followed, were ya?

LEWIS SWEGEL
You kiddin' me... We're professionals... Of course not...

TERRENCE MULLEN
Who's that ya brought with ya?

LEWIS SWEGEL
This here's the getaway driver I told you about, Billy Brown.

JACK HUGHES
How long have ya been a getaway driver there, Mr. Billy Brown?

BILLY BROWN
Well... It's hard to say but I--

TERRENCE MULLEN
Well, ya do have experience in getaway drivin' don'tcha?

BILLY BROWN
Why, of course I do...

JACK HUGHES
Maybe you tell us a little about
your experience... So we know
you're on the level.

BILLY BROWN
Well... See... The thing is...

TRAIN WHISTLE

TRAIN CONDUCTOR
All aboard that's comin' aboard...
Last call...

LEWIS SWEGEL
Look, save the interrogation for
the train ride... We better get on
board...

RUNNING FOOTSTEPS X2

LINCOLN GUARD OF HONOR
It was at this very moment when the
men boarded the front car of the
train that Tyrelle's men sprang
into action and boarded the last
car.

SECRET SERVICE AGENT
That's our cue men... The
informants have boarded the train
car with the grave robbers that
plan to disgrace the president's
good name... Let's hurry up and
casually board the last car...

TRAIN LEAVING THE STATION

INT. TRAIN

INTERIOR TAIN SFX

LINCOLN GUARD OF HONOR
Once they were upon the train, they
would go into detail as to how they
would go about stealing the body
and smuggling it north. To the
dunes on the shore of Lake
Michigan... This train ride would
take nine hours to complete...

                    SON
Nine hours on a train!

                    DAUGHTER
With no phone or t.v.? Gosh, that sounds boring.

                    LINCOLN GUARD OF HONOR
Well yes... It's easy to take for granted that today you can get from Springfield to Chicago in car in just three hours, in what those days took nine hours on a train... So you can only imagine how long a ride it would have been back in a horse drawn carriage with a coffin in the back...

                    FATHER
Probably two days... Wow... That's exciting stuff, huh kids?

                    SON
Shut up, dad...

                    DAUGHTER
Yeah, let him finish, dad.

                    LINCOLN GUARD OF HONOR
Anyways, it was on the long train ride that they would go over the details of Big Jim's plan...

                    TERRENCE MULLEN
So, Jim, when we get there, locate the tomb in the graveyard. And then while I cut through the lock, Billy, you go and steal us a getaway... Hopefully by the time you get back, we'll have broken into the tomb and be carrying Lincoln's coffin out.

                    LEWIS SWEGEL
Sounds pretty good... That's a pretty good plan. Only, if I would have came up with it, I would have came up with it better...

                    JACK HUGHES
How's that?

LEWIS SWEGEL
Well I would have had us get there yesterday. And in two different trains, at two different times. I also would have made sure I brought a hacksaw... You brought a hacksaw, didn't ya?

TERRENCE MULLEN
Nobody said anything to me about bringin' no hacksaw...

LEWIS SWEGEL
Oh you gotta be kidding me... What did ya bring?

JACK HUGHES
Well, we brought some files, didn't we...

LEWIS SWEGEL
I see... Well, that'll have to do... It's gonna take a lot longer but it'll work... I've stolen bodies with less...

TERRENCE MULLEN
Ya have, have ya?

LEWIS SWEGEL
Oh sure, how do you think I got the name Boss Body Snatcher of Chicago?

JACK HUGHES
How did ya get the name Boss Body Snatcher of Chicago?

TERRENCE MULLEN
Yeah... how did ya get the name, lad?

LEWIS SWEGEL
Look, that's not important... What is important is that you guys follow my lead and don't give me any guff... Billy and I have stolen many bodies. Don't you worry, you two, just worry about gettin' us in that tomb without anyone seeing us.

JACK HUGHES
And you two worry about stealing us a ride and loading that body up...

> JACK HUGHES
> Once we get back up north with it, "Big Jim" will know what to do next...

> LINCOLN GUARD OF HONOR
> Nine hours later the men would show up in Springfield, Illinois on the evening of November the 6th...

TRAIN ENTERING STATION
> Tyrrell and his agents followed the grave robbers overnight on the train and met with John Carroll Power, the custodian of Lincoln's tomb who agreed to help Tyrrell in the stakeout... On the evening of November the 7th, the first-ever secret service sting would go into effect.

FADE OUT TRAIN STATION

SCENE 6 EXT. OAKRIDGE CEMETERY

FADE IN CEMETERY NIGHT AMBIANCE

> LINCOLN GUARD OF HONOR
> Late at night in Oakridge Cemetery, Tyrrell and his men would wait in the vestibule near the tomb of Lincoln to catch the crooks in the act...

FADE IN GRAVE YARD SHIFT MUSIC

> PATRICK D. TYRRELL
> Ok men... We will wait down here until our informant gives us the code word to spring into action...

ECHOING FOOTSTEPS

> SECRET SERVICE AGENT
> Sounds like a good a plan...

> PATRICK D. TYRRELL
> Ok... Look, we can't be walkin' about down here with our shoes on... It'll blow our cover... Take off your shoes.

                    SECRET SERVICE AGENT
But sir... Then we would just be in
our stocking feet?

                    PATRICK D. TYRRELL
And, so?

                    SECRET SERVICE AGENT
Well, forgive me for speaking out
of line but don'tcha think that
we're gonna look a little silly in
our stocking feet trying to make a
federal arrest...

                    PATRICK D. TYRRELL
There's nothin' silly-looking about
protecting and honoring the late,
great President Lincoln... And if
your country requires you to prance
through the graveyard in your
stocking feet, well then, you get
to goin', shoeless lad.

                    SECRET SERVICE AGENT
Aye sir... You heard 'em... Take
yer shoes off, gents...

                                        SHOES FLOP OFF X4

                    LINCOLN GUARD OF HONOR
So, now that the Tyrrell and his
men are in their stocking feet,
they lay in wait to capture the
grave robbers on the other side of
the Oakridge Cemetery... Now,
something to keep in mind that was
working for the crooks-- One, there
was no night watchman... Two, there
was easy access to the sarcophagus
from outside the burial chamber.
And three... A padlock was all that
stood between them and entering the
tomb...

                                        FOOTSTEPS ON GRASS X2

                    TERRENCE MULLEN
Here we are, men... This is the
place.

                                        METAL PAD LOCK

                    JACK HUGHES
          And here's the lock... You were
          right, Swegel, we should have
          brought a hacksaw...

                    LEWIS SWEGEL
          Didn't I tell ya?

                    TERRENCE MULLEN
          Alright now, did ya bring the bag
          o' tools?...

                    JACK HUGHES
          'Course I brought the bag o'
          tools... That's my only job on this
          gig...

                                                    TOOL BAG THUMP
          Bring the bag o' tools and heft the
          coffin...

                    LEWIS SWEGEL
          And file that lock open, of
          course...

                    JACK HUGHES
          Is that so?

                    TERRENCE MULLEN
          Aye... That's so... I'm gonna keep
          an eye out this way... Swegel, you
          and Brown go the other way and get
          the buggy... Hughs, you commence to
          filing...

                    ALL 3
          Aye...

                    FOOTSTEPS AWAY ON GRASS

                                                    FILING METAL

                    LINCOLN GUARD OF HONOR
          So the 3 career criminals with no
          lock-picking experience whatsoever
          would saw at the padlock until it
          was open... This took over thirty
          minutes to accomplish...

                    LOCK OPEN
                                                    GATE CREEKING OPEN

                    LINCOLN GUARD OF HONOR
But once it was open, their
troubles were just beginning...

                    JACK HUGHES
It's finally open...

                    TERRENCE MULLEN
Good work... Look here comes Swegel
now.

                         FOOTSTEPS ON GRASS APPROACHING

                    LEWIS SWEGEL
Okay, Billy's in place with the
getaway carriage. You get that lock
open?

                    TERRENCE MULLEN
Aye... the sarcophagus is just
through here...

                    FOOTSTEPS IN CHAMBER X3
                              ADD REVERE TO VOICES

                    LEWIS SWEGEL
There he is ... Honest Abe

                    TERRENCE MULLEN
Honest Abe my tuchas... Hughes,
smash it open with the axe...

                    JACK HUGHES
Hmmmpf...

                    LEWIS SWEGEL
Woah... Wait, wait, wait... What
are you doin'... This is imported
Italian marble... Very expensive...
And LOUD if you crack it open with
an axe... There's gotta be a better
way... Put that axe down...

                                        AXE THUD

Here... Give me that crow-bar...
Look ... It's sealed with plaster
of Paris... We can pry it open.

                    PRYING SFX
                  STONE CRACKING SFX
                   LEWIS STRUGGLING
                  TERRENCE STRUGGLING
                                        JACK STRUGGLING

                    TERRENCE MULLEN
          Set... It... Over... Here... Ah...
          There... C'mon let us hoist the
          coffin out now...

                    JACK STRUGGLING
                    TERRENCE STRUGGLING
                                        LEWIS STRUGGLING

                    LEWIS SWEGEL
          Ahhh... It's no use, we can't even
          budge it...

                    JACK HUGHES
          There's no more than an inch for me
          to get my fingers in.

                    TERRENCE MULLEN
          It's absurdly heavy... Must weigh
          over 500 pounds...

                    LEWIS SWEGEL
          It's probably lined with lead...

                    TERRENCE MULLEN
          Go ahead, Jack, saw the footer off
          the sarcophagus...

                    JACK HUGHES
          Aye...

                    LEWIS SWEGEL
          What?!

                    TERRENCE MULLEN
          You're not gonna give up now, are
          ya Mr. Boss Body Snatcher?

                    LEWIS SWEGEL
          No.. Of course not... I was just
          gonna say the same thing... I tell
          ya what, once ya get that hacked
          off I'll run and grab Brown with
          the getaway buggy...

                    TERRENCE MULLEN
          Aye... Jack... commence to sawin'.

                                        STONE SAWING

                    LINCOLN GUARD OF HONOR
          This took another thirty minutes.
          But once the foot of the

                    LINCOLN GUARD OF HONOR
sarcophagus was cut off, Mullen and
Hughes would send Swegel to get
Billy Brown and the cart.

                    CUT SAWING
                                    STONE ON STONE THUD

                    JACK HUGHES
There... It's off... We should be
able to drag it free...

                    TERRENCE MULLEN
Swegel... Go get Mr. Billy Brown
and the cart... It's gonna take all
four of us to heft this coffin...

                    LEWIS SWEGEL
Aye...

                                    FOOTSTEPS ON GRASS AWAY

                    LINCOLN GUARD OF HONOR
Now, Mullen and Hughes sent Swegel
to retrieve the wagon, but instead
Swegel tipped off the waiting law
enforcement officials in the
vestibule of the tomb.

                                    FOOTSTEPS APPROACHING

                    SECRET SERVICE AGENT
I think I hear something...

                    LEWIS SWEGEL
WASH...

                    LINCOLN GUARD OF HONOR
Finally, Swegel gave the
pre-arranged code word, "wash,"
which sent the agents into action!

                    PATRICK D. TYRRELL
That's the word, men, let's go...

                    SECRET SERVICE AGENT
Wait, we're still in our stocking
feet... couldn't we put our shoes
on before we get into a foot
chase...

                    PATRICK D. TYRRELL
Damn you and your dry feet... A
real Secret Service agent can catch
a crook in his socks... Now get in
there and make an arrest... That's
an order...

                    SECRET SERVICE AGENT
Aye Captain... Alright men, you
heard him, let's go... But go
quietly until the last second...
Now go, go, go...

                    FOOTSTEPS ON GRASS
                                                    DRAMATIC SWELL

                    LINCOLN GUARD OF HONOR
Now when Tyrrell's men spring into
action, they lose eachother in the
dark of the cemetery... And, well,
guns weren't so reliable, and while
sneaking across the cemetery, one
of the pinkerton's guns went off...
And, well, you can imagine a
gunshot from a gun built in 1876,
in the middle of a quiet graveyard
sounded like a cannon firing.

                                                    SINGLE CANNON FIRE

                    TERRENCE MULLEN
What was that?

                    JACK HUGHES
Oh my God... They must have got
Swegel...

                    TERRENCE MULLEN
I think we've been discovered
lad... We better make a run for
it... Grab your revolver at the
ready.

                    JACK HUGHES
What about Swegel?

                    TERRENCE MULLEN
We'll mourn for him... C'mon let's
go...

                                                    RUNNING AWAY

> **LINCOLN GUARD OF HONOR**
> Of course, as soon as Mullen and Hughes heard the gunshot they made a beeline out of the cemetery and back to Chicago just as fast as they could... However, Tyrrell got separated from his pinkertons in the dark and started to return fire.

CANNON FIRE

> **SECRET SERVICE AGENT**
> What... Who the hell shooting?... Return fire!

MULTIPUL GUN FIRE

> **PATRICK D. TYRRELL**
> Stop... In the name of the law... You're under arrest by United States Secret Service!

MORE GUN FIRE

> **SECRET SERVICE AGENT**
> Is that the Captain?... Wait a minute... Cease fire!.. Cease fire!

CUT OUT GUN SHOTS

> Captain?... Is that you?

FADE OUT DRAMATIC MUSIC

> **PATRICK D. TYRRELL**
> Indeed?... Who goes there?

> **SECRET SERVICE AGENT**
> It's me, and the other pinkertons... Who are you firing at?

> **PATRICK D. TYRRELL**
> Well, who are you firing at?

> **SECRET SERVICE AGENT**
> Well, I thought I was shooting at the graverobbers...

> **PATRICK D. TYRRELL**
> I, too, thought I was shooting at the graverobbers... Are you telling me we have no graverobbers to shoot at?

                    SECRET SERVICE AGENT
It would appear that way,
Captain...

                                        LEAVES RUSTLING

                    PATRICK D. TYRRELL
What's that... Who goes there?

                    LEWIS SWEGEL
It's just me... Don't shoot..

                    SECRET SERVICE AGENT
It's informant Lewis Swegel,
Captain...

                    PATRICK D. TYRRELL
Swegel... Is that you, boy? Come
here...

                                        FOOTSTEPS APPROACHING

                    LEWIS SWEGEL
I heard gunfire and I hit the
deck... What's with all the
shooting?

                    PATRICK D. TYRRELL
Where is Mullen and Hughes?!

                    LEWIS SWEGEL
Well, they made a break for it when
they heard the gunfire... What's
with all the shooting in the dark?

                    SECRET SERVICE AGENT
Uh... That was my fault... Ya
see... I ran off half-cocked and,
well, I took a bit of a stumble
running through the cemetery and my
gun discharged...

                    PATRICK D. TYRRELL
Cursed luck... Well... I imagine
Big Jim Kennally's men will come
running right back to him... We
should make our way back to Chicago
...

                    LEWIS SWEGEL
Can I ask you guys something... Why
are you out here in your stocking
feet?

SECRET SERVICE AGENT
Yeah? why are we out here in our stocking feet captain?

PATRICK D. TYRRELL
For Justice...

BILLY BROWN
Psst.... Hey...

PATRICK D. TYRRELL
Who's that?...

BILLY BROWN
It's me, Billy Brown... Don't shoot...

PATRICK D. TYRRELL
Brown! Come here at once!

FOOTSTEPS ON GRASS

BILLY BROWN
I saw Terrence and Hughes run that way towards the train station

SECRET SERVICE AGENT
Sounds like you were right, Captain...

PATRICK D. TYRRELL
Of course... Let's make our way back to Chicago at once...

BILLY BROWN
Wait a minute... Why is everyone shoeless? Did I miss something?

LINCOLN GUARD OF HONOR
And sooo... Tyrrell and his agents failed to arrest Mullen and Hughes that night. However, they would succeed a week later back in Chicago. Back at the tavern known as The Hub...

FADE OUT ENVIRONMENT

SCENE 7 THE HUB SEVERAL WEEKS LATER

> FADE IN "THE HUB MUSIC"
> SALOON DOORS SWINGING
> COWBOY BOOTS ON WOOD FLOOR

LINCOLN GUARD OF HONOR
You see, Tyrrell was right... Big Jim's men came running back to him to tell him of the foiled attempt to steal Lincoln's body... Tyrrell and his agents would track them all the way back to The Hub to find Mullen working the bar, and Big Jim sleeping in the corner by the pot-bellied stove...

SECRET SERVICE AGENT
Barkeep... Two Ales for us, please.

TERRENCE MULLEN
Aye...

LINCOLN GUARD OF HONOR
As soon as Mullen turned around with the beers, Tyrrell drew his pistol on him and said:

PATRICK D. TYRRELL
You're mine, Terrence Mullen...

SECRET SERVICE AGENT
Rise and shine, Big Jim... You're under arrest... For the attempted kidnapping of former President Lincoln's body.

BIG JIM
How do you figure? I haven't left Chicago in months...

SECRET SERVICE AGENT
We have testimonies that will put all of you away and reunite you with your friend Benjamin Boyd...

LINCOLN GUARD OF HONOR
And he was right... Terrence Mullen and Jack Hughes and Big Jim Kennally would all be convicted of their crimes and sentenced to time in jail, based on Lewis Swegel and Billy Brown's testimony... And that

> LINCOLN GUARD OF HONOR
> was the first mission that the Secret Service was given that required they protect a President's body... Even if it was already dead!

> FADE OUT "THE HUB" ENVIRONMENT

SCENE 8 EXT. THE LINCOLN MONUMENT

> FADE IN OUT DOOR PUBLIC PARK

> LINCOLN GUARD OF HONOR
> And that is how the first-ever Secret Service sting was executed...

> SON
> But wait... What happened to Lincoln's body?

> LINCOLN GUARD OF HONOR
> That's a verrry good question... You've been listening haven't you... Well... That's this whole crazy thing too... You see, the way Lincoln's coffin and sarcophagus was damaged and partially exposed was too much for the custodian John Carroll Power to fix... So he had Tyrrell and his agents drag the coffin to the basement of the monument and cover it with rubbish and debris...

> DAUGHTER
> Wait you mean his coffin was hidden in some trash for years???

> LINCOLN GUARD OF HONOR
> That's right!... The only person outside of their inner circle who knew, was Lincoln's last surviving child, Robert Todd Lincoln.

> SON
> So how long was he all hidden in the rubbish?

> LINCOLN GUARD OF HONOR
> Till July 1882, after Mary Lincoln died... They remained in the basement together until 1887.

DAUGHTER
Where is his body now?

LINCOLN GUARD OF HONOR
In 1887 Lincoln and his wife were encased in a brick vault and buried under ten feet of concrete below our very feet...

SON
How can you be so sure his body is in there?

LINCOLN GUARD OF HONOR
To ensure Lincoln's remains were still there, the coffin was opened by the Guard of Honor, who saw that, indeed, it was Lincoln in the coffin.

SON
What's the Guard of Honor?

LINCOLN GUARD OF HONOR
On February 12, 1880, on what would have been Lincoln's 71st birthday, the former custodian Power and his associates formed the "Lincoln Guard of Honor," to serve as the custodians of Lincoln's body, keeping the President's remains hidden, which has now been proudly passed on to me...

SON
You mean you're a custodian?

DAUGHTER
We just listened to this whole story from a custodian?

LINCOLN GUARD OF HONOR
I am a Lincoln Guard of Honor... And it's a very good job...

SON
Yeah right!... You're full of it! I don't believe any of that now.

DAUGHTER
Yeah, fat chance...

> LINCOLN GUARD OF HONOR
> It's a true story, I swear to it!

> FATHER
> C'mon kids, let's go before he turns the lights out on us...

FOOTSTEPS SCURRY AWAY

> LINCOLN GUARD OF HONOR
> I am a Guard of Honor...

SON AND DAUGHTER LAUGHING IN THE DISTANCE

> SON
> (yelling from a distance)
> I'm not sorry I called you a snore monger!

SON LAUGHING

> LINCOLN GUARD OF HONOR
> I'm not just a custodian!... I guard the remains of former President Lincoln... ... and his honor...

FADE OUT ENVIRONMENT

CREDITS

FADE IN OUTRO MUSIC

> THE VOICE OF THE CLEVELAND RADIO PLAYERS
> You have been listening to The Cleveland Radio Players' performance of Stealing Lincoln. Written by Milton Matthew Horowitz... Narrated by Jack Matuszewski,... Starring:

GIOVANNI CASTIGLIONE

LLINNELLE GIBSON

TYLER MOLITERNO

CODY ZACK

CHARLES HARGRAVE

ROBBERT BRANCH

DAVID FLYNT

CORY SHY

LOGAN SMITH
and my name is Denny Castiglone, ladies and gentlemen... Stealing Lincoln was Recorded live in one take at Bad Racket Studios... Made in part by Gotta Groove Records. To purchase Stealing Lincoln as a radio play on MP3, Audio Book, paperback, or E-book please visit www.clevelandradioplayers.com Copyright 2015.

FADE ALL

END

Rights and Royalties

Originally adapted for the radio and performed by The Cleveland Radio Players

Directed by Milton Matthew Horowitz

Recorded at Bad Racket Studios

For more information on performance rights and royalties, or to listen to Stealing Lincoln as a radio play, please visit www.ClevelandRadioPlayers.com